SPOTLIGHT ON SOCIAL AND EMOTIONAL LEARNING

BELIEVING IN YOURSELF

ACHIEVING CONFIDENCE

THERESA EMMINIZER

PowerKiDS press

NEW YORK

Published in 2020 by The Rosen Publishing Group, Inc.
29 East 21st Street, New York, NY 10010

Editor: Elizabeth Krajnik
Designer: Michael Flynn

Photo Credits: Cover artpipi/E+/Getty Images; cover 1, 2–3, 4, 6, 8, 10, 12–14, 16, 18–24 (background) TairA/Shutterstock.com; p. 5 Courtesy of the Library of Congress; p. 7 Peter M. Fisher/Corbis/Getty Images; p. 9 UniversalImagesGroup/Getty Images; p. 11 Marilyn Nieves/E+/Getty Images; p. 12 Jacek Chabraszewski/Shutterstock.com; p. 13 LightField Studios/Shutterstock.com; p. 15 tatyana_aleksieva/RooM/Getty Images; p. 17 KidStock/Blend Images/Getty Images; p. 18 Syda Productions/Shutterstock.com; p. 19 Craig Barritt/Getty Images Entertainment/Getty Images; p. 20 https://commons.wikimedia.org/wiki/File:Zhang_Lu-Laozi_Riding_an_Ox.jpg; p. 21 Steve Allen/Shutterstock.com; p. 22 Suzanne Tucker/Shutterstock.com.

Cataloging-in-Publication Data

Names: Emminizer, Theresa.
Title: Believing in yourself: achieving confidence / Theresa Emminizer.
Description: New York : PowerKids Press, 2020. | Series: Spotlight on social and emotional learning | Includes glossary and index.
Identifiers: ISBN 9781725302129 (pbk.) | ISBN 9781725301900 (library bound) | ISBN 9781725301894 (6pack)
Subjects: LCSH: Self-confidence--Juvenile literature.
Classification: LCC BJ1533.S27 E46 2020 | DDC 158.1--dc23

Manufactured in the United States of America

CPSIA Compliance Information: Batch #CSPK19. For further information contact Rosen Publishing, New York, New York at 1-800-237-9932.

CONTENTS

CHAPTER ONE

WHAT IS CONFIDENCE?

The word "confidence" comes from the Latin word *fidere*, which means "to trust." Confidence is having trust in oneself. It isn't thinking that you're better than others. It's believing that you're capable of dealing with whatever challenges might come your way. Confidence gives you the strength to **cope** with **difficult** situations, try new things, and enjoy your life. To a confident person, the world is an exciting place that's full of possibilities!

Confidence isn't something only certain people are born with. It's not a skill or a behavior. It's a state of mind. Everyone is capable of becoming a confident person. Anyone can learn to **develop** self-confidence through practice. Our emotional, physical, and social well-being all contribute to confidence. Even the most insecure person can build confidence by shifting their mindset, pushing their boundaries, and embracing their individuality.

Michelle Obama, pictured here, said, "Through my education, I didn't just develop skills, I didn't just develop the ability to learn, but I developed confidence."

CHAPTER TWO

OWN YOUR STRENGTHS

It's easy to compare yourself to others. But, in truth, no one is better than you and no one is worse than you. Every person is unique, or one of a kind. There will always be someone who plays an instrument more skillfully, someone who is better dressed, or someone who is funnier. However, it's important to remember that another person's strengths don't reflect badly on you. Someone else's successes aren't your failures. What's important is to identify your own strengths and **cultivate** them!

A key part of confidence is being self-aware. What makes you feel good about yourself? Maybe you're a talented painter or a good listener. No matter how big or small it is, think of something you like about yourself and take a moment to **appreciate** it. Recognizing your strengths will help you build confidence.

Social media can encourage competing with others for approval. But the number of "likes" someone gets doesn't help their confidence. Confidence comes from inner security.

CHAPTER THREE

FACE YOUR FEARS

Courage doesn't mean not being afraid. It means working through your fears and not allowing them to stop you from living your life. Courage and confidence go hand in hand. A good way to build confidence is to do something you're afraid of. This doesn't mean you have to go skydiving or ride on a motorcycle! Just stepping outside your comfort zone is enough.

Maybe you aren't very **coordinated** and feel uncomfortable in gym class. Instead of getting a note excusing you from class, try showing up and doing your best. It doesn't matter if you aren't as **athletic** as some of your classmates. Each time you do something you're afraid of, you'll feel a little bit more confident because you know you're stronger than your fears. The more you do, the more you're capable of doing!

Eleanor Roosevelt, pictured here, said, "You gain strength, courage, and confidence by every experience in which you really stop to look fear in the face."

CHAPTER FOUR

THE POWER OF VISUALIZATION

Having a feeling of control over your life can help you feel more confident. If you're unhappy with the way things are, you can empower, or give power to, yourself by visualizing a better future. This means forming a picture in your mind.

A vision board is a fun tool to help you come up with specific goals for your future. First, you'll need a blank board made of cardboard, wood, or cork. Looking at your empty board, think about how you want to feel. What concrete changes can you make to improve your confidence? Maybe you love to sing but are too shy to do it in public. Could trying out for the school musical help you face your fears and build confidence? Cut out a magazine photo or print a picture that represents that goal and put it on your vision board. You can bring to life the things you visualize.

The pictures on your board can help you visualize your dreams and inspire you to turn them into realities.

CHAPTER FIVE

FOCUS ON SUCCESS

How can you meet the goals you lay out for yourself? First, make sure they're practical and **achievable**. Don't set goals for yourself that are too big. Choose goals that you know you can accomplish. For example, if you want to become a better student but have trouble getting homework done on time, just focus on that to start. You don't have to focus on having the highest grade in your class.

Most goals aren't accomplished overnight. They take time, effort, and a lot of patience.

Then, recognize the progress you make along the way. Every day you finish your assignments on time, take a moment to feel proud of yourself. Each small achievement brings you closer to achieving your end goal.

If you don't meet all your goals, it doesn't mean you're a failure. Some goals take longer to achieve than others. Confidence comes from taking pride in your efforts and having faith that you're always growing and improving.

CHAPTER SIX

MAKE TIME FOR SELF-CARE

Taking care of your body can help you build confidence. Exercise can help take your mind off what's troubling you. It can also make you feel strong and accomplished. More importantly, connecting with your body can make you feel more grounded and secure. However, you don't have to be super fit to feel good about yourself.

Recognize what your body needs and make sure you're getting it. It's hard to feel confident when you're hungry or haven't slept! Self-care could mean eating a healthy meal, stretching your muscles, or even just brushing your hair. Taking time for these little acts of self-care can help give you a sense of calm and confidence in your busy day-to-day life. When you feel well cared for, you feel more confident and ready to take on the world.

You could practice self-care by taking time to go outside or doing breathing exercises.

CHAPTER SEVEN

LEND A HELPING HAND

Just as stepping out of your comfort zone can help you develop self-confidence, so can stepping outside of yourself! When you feel bad, it can be easy to **fixate** on all the things you wish were different. Shifting your focus outside yourself can help you gain perspective, or a point of view.

Many people feel worried or upset by problems going on in the world around them. This might make them feel powerless. You can build confidence by taking an active role, or part, to help solve the problems that worry you. You could take part in a food drive, visit a nursing home, or clean up litter. You could make it a goal to do one kind act for another person every day. Contributing to a cause you believe in makes you feel good about your place in the world. This increases your sense of self-worth.

Volunteering at a soup kitchen is a good way to help others. You can help cook food, pass out plates, or even do dishes in the back if you're shy.

Ariana

CHAPTER EIGHT

DO WHAT WORKS

Is there an activity that makes you feel strong and confident? Maybe you pump yourself up for a big event by blasting your favorite song and dancing in your bedroom. Maybe you pose like a superhero and walk out your door with your head held high. Or maybe you look at your reflection in the mirror and repeat a positive phrase, such as, "I am unstoppable!"

Amy Cuddy, pictured here, is a **psychologist** who popularized the idea of "power posing" to build confidence. Some people find power posing to be very helpful.

Many people use positive affirmations to help them build confidence. Positive affirmations are phrases designed to help people overcome **negative** thoughts. Some positive affirmations are specific to challenges in a person's life. For example, if someone struggles with anxiety, their affirmation might be, "I am calm. I am in control."

There are many ways to boost your confidence. Don't be afraid to embrace whatever tool works best for you!

CHAPTER NINE

BE TRUE TO YOU

Lao-tzu, an early Chinese **philosopher**, once wrote: "Because one believes in oneself, one doesn't try to convince others. Because one is content with oneself, one doesn't need others' approval. Because one accepts oneself, the whole world accepts him or her."

Being authentic, or true to oneself, isn't easy. Most people have insecurities and are afraid of being judged by others. You might feel **self-conscious** about your braces, so you hide your teeth when you smile. But Lao-tzu suggests that if you accept yourself completely—flaws and all—others will too!

Lao-tzu, pictured here, was the father of Taoism, which is a way of thinking that places a great deal of importance on living simply and honestly and in harmony with nature.

Remind yourself that perfection is boring. Our **idiosyncrasies** are what make us interesting. Embracing your imperfections will help you—and others—appreciate what makes you special. When you stop trying so hard to be perfect, you'll spend less time worrying about what others think about you and more time having fun!

CHAPTER TEN

WHY CONFIDENCE MATTERS

Confidence isn't always easy to come by, but it's well worth the effort. When we lack confidence, we often limit ourselves and try to hide our imperfections. Our fear of failure or disappointment keeps us from taking part in the world in a healthy way.

Confidence makes it possible to put yourself out there. With more confidence you'll try new things, build positive relationships, succeed in school, and enjoy life to the fullest. However, confidence isn't achieved by being the smartest student, the best athlete, or the most popular person. True confidence comes from accepting yourself, valuing your unique strengths, and trusting your ability to overcome challenges.

Sometimes confidence requires a lot of effort. But small steps can make a big difference in changing your thoughts and growing to have a confident state of mind. Start by asking yourself, "What do I like best about being me?"

GLOSSARY

achievable (uh-CHEE-vuh-buhl) Able to be obtained by means of hard work.

appreciate (uh-PREE-shee-ayt) To understand something's worth or value.

athletic (ath-LEH-tik) Active in sports or exercises, or strong and muscular.

coordinated (koh-OR-duh-nay-tuhd) Able to use more than one set of muscle movements to a single end.

cope (KOHP) To deal with and try to find solutions for problems.

cultivate (KUHL-tuh-vayt) To grow and care for something.

develop (dih-VEHL-uhp) To bring out the possibilities of, to begin to have gradually, or to create over time.

difficult (DIH-fih-kuhlt) Hard to do, make, or carry out.

fixate (FIK-sayt) To look at or think about something constantly.

idiosyncrasy (ih-dee-uh-SIN-kruh-see) An unusual way in which a particular person behaves or thinks.

negative (NEH-guh-tiv) Harmful or bad, also unwanted.

philosopher (fuh-LAH-suh-fuhr) A person who studies philosophy, or the study of the basic ideas about knowledge, right and wrong, reasoning, and the value of things.

psychologist (sy-KAH-luh-jist) Someone who studies psychology, or the science of the mind and behavior.

self-conscious (sehlf–KAHN-shuhs) Feeling uncomfortably nervous or embarrassed when in the presence of or when being observed by other people.

INDEX

PRIMARY SOURCE LIST

Page 5
First Lady Michelle Obama official portrait. Photograph. Joyce N. Boghosian. February 18, 2009. Now held at the Library of Congress Prints and Photographs Division, Washington, D.C.

Page 9
Eleanor Roosevelt in front of the White House. Photograph. Universal Images Group. January 1943.

Page 20
Laozi Riding an Ox. Painting. Zhang Lu. ca. Ming Dynasty, 1368–1644. Now held at the National Palace Museum, Taipei, Taiwan.

WEBSITES

Due to the changing nature of Internet links, PowerKids Press has developed an online list of websites related to the subject of this book. This site is updated regularly. Please use this link to access the list: www.powerkidslinks.com/SSEL/yourself